Say the name of each picture. Circle each picture that begins with the **b** sound.

Say the name of each picture. Draw a line from the barn to each picture that begins with the **b** sound.

CD-104343

Trace each letter c. Circle the picture in each row whose name begins with the hard c sound.

CD-104343

3

Say the name of each picture. Draw an X on each picture that begins with the hard c sound.

CD-104343

Say the name of each picture. Circle each picture that begins with the d sound.

Say the name of each picture. Draw a line from the dog to each picture that begins with the d sound.

CD-104343 © Carson-Dellosa

Say the name of each picture. Circle the picture in each row that begins with the f sound.

Say the name of each picture. Circle each picture that begins with the **f** sound.

CD-104343

Say the name of each picture. Circle each picture that begins with the hard g sound.

Say the name of each picture. Draw a line from the gorilla to each picture that begins with the hard g sound.

CD-104343

Say the name of each picture. Circle the letter of the beginning sound.

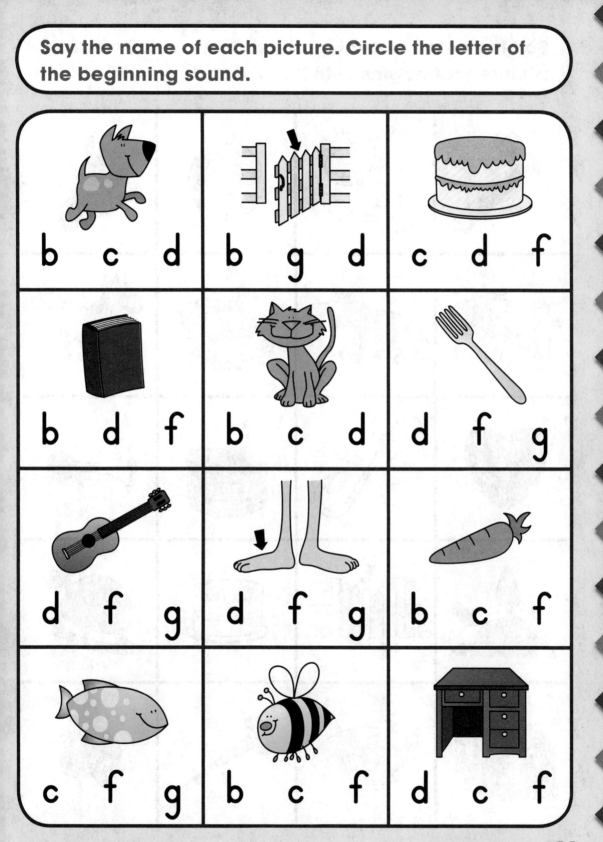

b　c　d   b　g　d   c　d　f

b　d　f   b　c　d   d　f　g

d　f　g   d　f　g   b　c　f

c　f　g   b　c　f   d　c　f

　　　　CD-104343　　**11**

Say the name of each picture. Draw an X on each picture that begins with the h sound.

CD-104343 © Carson-Dellosa

Say the name of each picture. Color the picture in each box that begins with the h sound.

Say the name of each picture. Circle each picture that begins with the j sound.

Say the name of each picture. Draw a line from the jet to each picture that begins with the j sound.

Say the name of each picture. Circle each picture that begins with the **k** sound.

CD-104343

Say the name of each picture. Draw a line from the kite to each picture that begins with the k sound.

Trace each letter l. Circle the picture in each row whose name begins with the l sound.

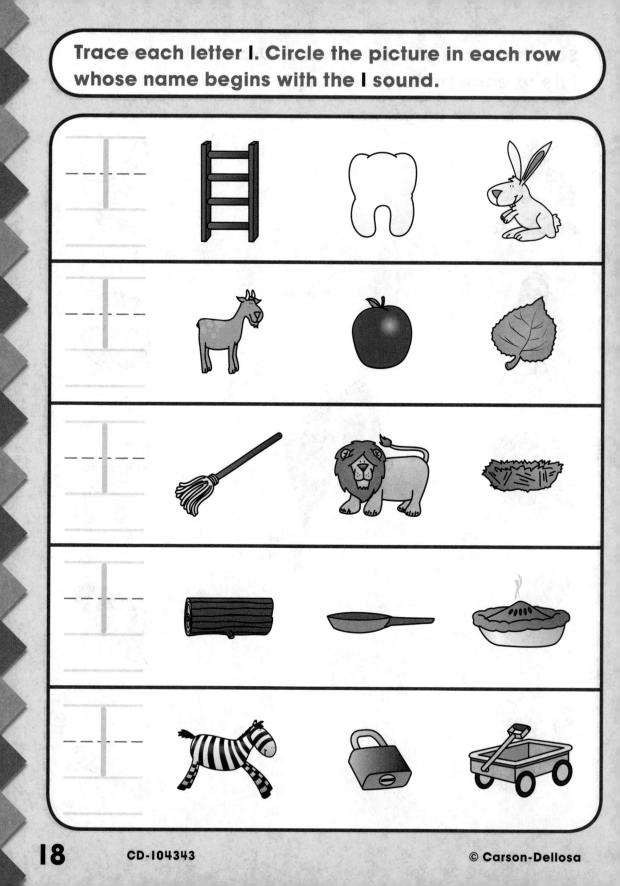

CD-104343

Say the name of each picture. Draw an X on each picture that begins with the l sound.

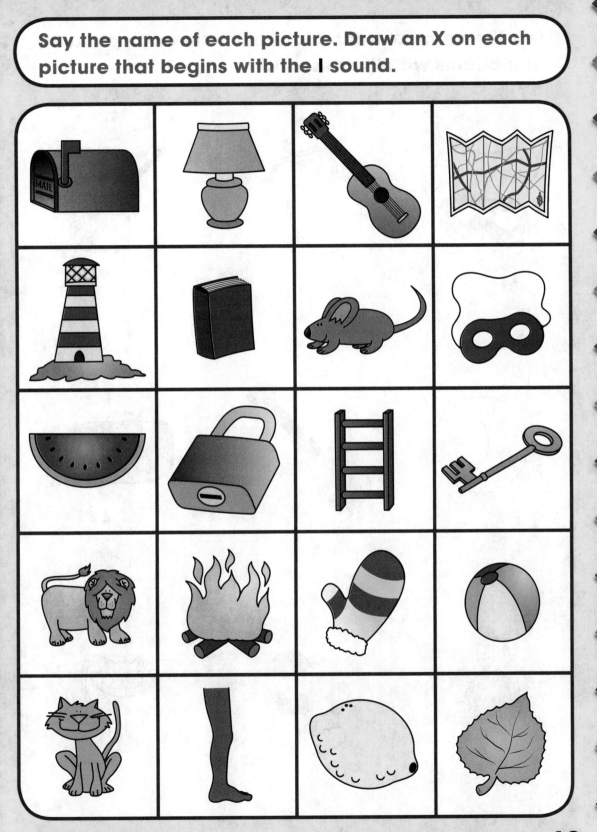

Say the name of each picture. Circle each picture that begins with the **m** sound.

CD-104343 © Carson-Dellosa

Say the name of each picture. Draw a line from the moon to each picture that begins with the m sound.

Say the name of each picture. Draw a line from the nut to each picture that begins with the n sound.

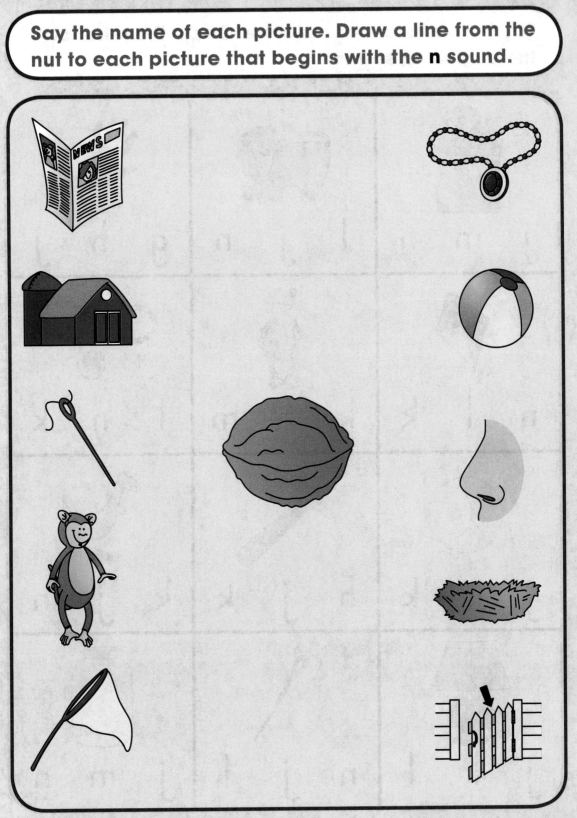

Say the name of each picture. Circle the letter of the beginning sound.

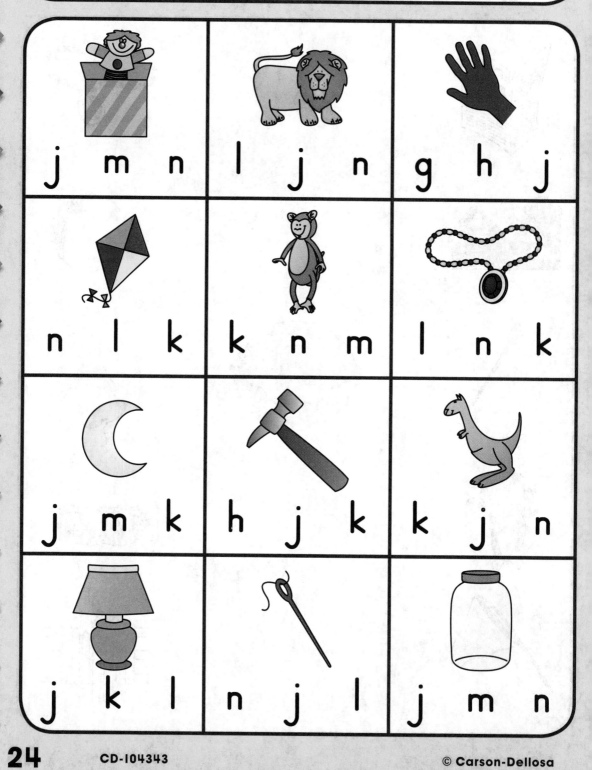

j m n

l j n

g h j

n l k

k n m

l n k

j m k

h j k

k j n

j k l

n j l

j m n

CD-104343   © Carson-Dellosa

Say the name of each picture. Circle each picture that begins with the p sound.

Trace each letter p. Circle the picture in each row whose name begins with the p sound.

CD-104343   © Carson-Dellosa

Trace each letter q. Circle the picture in each row whose name begins with the letter q.

Say the name of each picture. Circle each picture that begins with the r sound.

Trace each letter r. Circle the picture in each row whose name begins with the r sound.

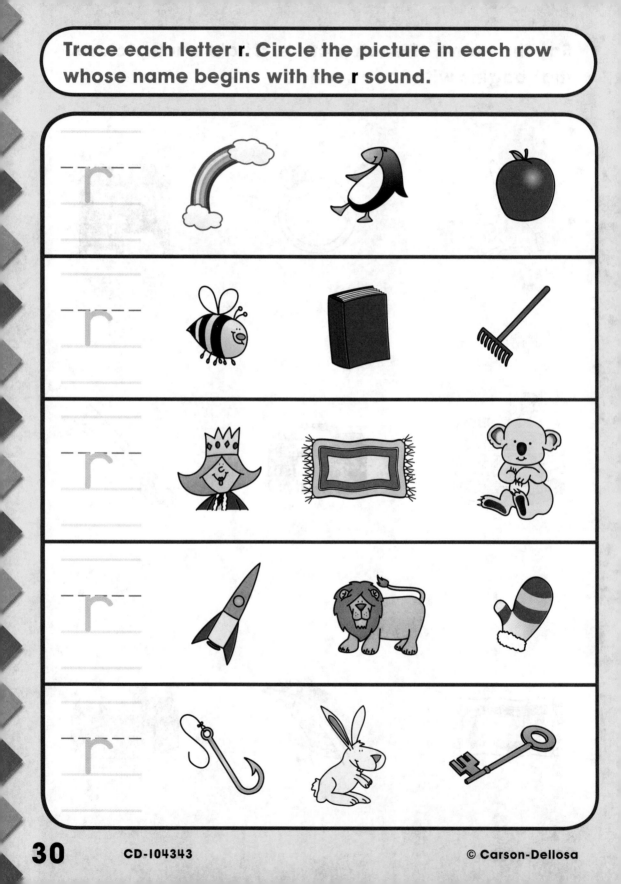

CD-104343 © Carson-Dellosa

Page 1
The boat, banana, ball, butterfly, and bee should be circled.

Page 2
Lines should be drawn from the barn to the book, bat, bib, ball, and balloon.

Page 3
The letters should be traced.
Row 1: cake; Row 2: carrot;
Row 3: cat; Row 4: car;
Row 5: can

Page 4
Row 1: car, cow
Row 2: camera, cookie
Row 3: cake, carrot
Row 4: cat, corn
Row 5: can, cane, comb

Page 5
The doll, dinosaur, dice, door, dog, and duck should be circled.

Page 6
Lines should be drawn from the dog to the duck, dice, desk, dinosaur, and door.

Page 7
Row 1: feather; Row 2: fan;
Row 3: fork; Row 4: fox;
Row 5: fish

Page 8
The foot, fork, fire, five, and fish should be circled.

Page 9
The gate, gum, goose, guitar, and goat should be circled.

Page 10
Lines should be drawn from the gorilla to the gate, goose, goat, girl, goal, and guitar.

Page 11
Row 1: d, g, c
Row 2: b, c, f
Row 3: g, f, c
Row 4: f, b, d

Page 12
Row 1: hammer, hand
Row 2: hippo, horse
Row 3: heart, hook, hose, horn
Row 4: hill, hat
Row 5: house

Page 13
The horse, horn, hand, and hammer should be colored.

Page 14
The jellyfish, jack-in-the-box, jam, jar, and jacks should be circled.

Page 15
Lines should be drawn from the jet to the jellyfish, jack-in-the-box, jug, jar, and jacks.

Page 16
The king, kite, kangaroo, and key should be circled.

Page 17
Lines should be drawn from
the kite to the king, koala,
kangaroo, and key.

Page 18
The letters should be traced.
Row 1: ladder; Row 2: leaf;
Row 3: lion; Row 4: log;
Row 5: lock

Page 19
Row 1: lamp
Row 2: lighthouse
Row 3: lock, ladder
Row 4: lion
Row 5: leg, lemon, leaf

Page 20
The mask, mop, moon, mailbox,
monkey, and mitten should be
circled.

Page 21
Lines should be drawn from the
moon to the map, mouse, mop,
mailbox, and mask.

Page 22
The newspaper, needle,
necklace, net, and nest should
be circled.

Page 23
Lines should be drawn from the
nut to the newspaper, needle,
net, necklace, nose, and nest.

Page 24
Row 1: j, l, h
Row 2: k, m, n
Row 3: m, h, k
Row 4: l, n, j

Page 25
The pie, pan, pizza, pumpkin,
penguin, and pen should be
circled.

Page 26
The letters should be traced.
Row 1: pizza; Row 2: pencil;
Row 3: penguin; Row 4: pan;
Row 5: pie

Page 27
The letters should be traced.
Row 1: quail; Row 2: quarter;
Row 3: quilt; Row 4: queen;
Row 5: question mark

Page 28
Lines should be drawn from the
queen to the question mark,
quarter, quail, and quilt.

Page 29
The rabbit, ring, rope, ruler, and
rug should be circled.

Page 30
The letters should be traced.
Row 1: rainbow; Row 2: rake;
Row 3: rug; Row 4: rocket;
Row 5: rabbit

Page 31
The sun, sock, sink, and saw
should be circled.

Page 32
Row 1: soap, sub, sandwich
Row 2: saw, seven
Row 3: sink, six, soup
Row 4: sand, seal
Row 5: sun, seesaw, sock

Page 33
The turtle, tooth, tiger, and tent should be circled.

Page 34
Lines should be drawn from the tiger to the tent, tape, top, tooth, and turtle.

Page 35
The vase, vacuum cleaner, volcano, vest, and violin should be circled.

Page 36
Lines should be drawn from the vase to the volcano, vacuum cleaner, valentine, vest, and violin.

Page 37
Row 1: r, t, p
Row 2: s, v, q
Row 3: p, t, r
Row 4: s, q, v

Page 38
The watermelon, wig, web, wagon, and walrus should be circled.

Page 39
Lines should be drawn from the walrus to the web, window, watermelon, watch, and windmill.

Page 40
The letters should be traced.
Row 1: yo-yo; Row 2: yellow;
Row 3: yak; Row 4: yarn;
Row 5: yolk

Page 41
The yarn, yellow, yak, yolk, and yo-yo should be circled.

Page 42
The zebra, zipper, and zero should be circled.

Page 43
Lines should be drawn from the zebra to the zero, zipper, and zoo.

Page 44
Row 1: k, n
Row 2: w, b
Row 3: t, d
Row 4: h, z

Page 45
Row 1: p, m
Row 2: v, g
Row 3: j, y
Row 4: s, l

Page 46
The map, cat, fan, hat, and can should be circled.

Page 47
Row 1: flag, map
Row 2: hat, tag, fan
Row 3: lamp, mask, man

Page 48
Row 1: cap, can, hat
Row 2: bag, mask, lamp
Row 3: bat, tag, ham

Page 49
The bell, pen, desk, net, tent, and nest should be circled.

Page 50
Row 1: bed, leg
Row 2: jet, pen, vest
Row 3: tent, net, bell

Page 51
Row 1: pen, dress, net
Row 2: sled, bell, desk
Row 3: leg, tent, vest

Page 52
The fish, pin, wig, bib, and six should be circled.

Page 53
Row 1: kit, pin
Row 2: fish, king, dish
Row 3: chin, wig, six

Page 54
Row 1: fish, pin, lips
Row 2: king, chin, sink
Row 3: six, wing, wig

Page 55
The fox, mop, doll, log, dog, and sock should be circled.

Page 56
Row 1: top, pot
Row 2: fox, dog, lock
Row 3: mop, log, doll

Page 57
Row 1: lock, block, dog
Row 2: sock, mop, top
Row 3: frog, log, pot

Page 58
The rug, duck, gum, and sun should be circled.

Page 59
Row 1: rug, tub
Row 2: sun, drum, nut
Row 3: duck, hut, mug

Page 60
Row 1: hut, rug, mug
Row 2: sun, duck, gum
Row 3: nut, drum, jug

Say the name of each picture. Circle each picture that begins with the s sound.

Say the name of each picture. Draw an X on each picture that begins with the s sound.

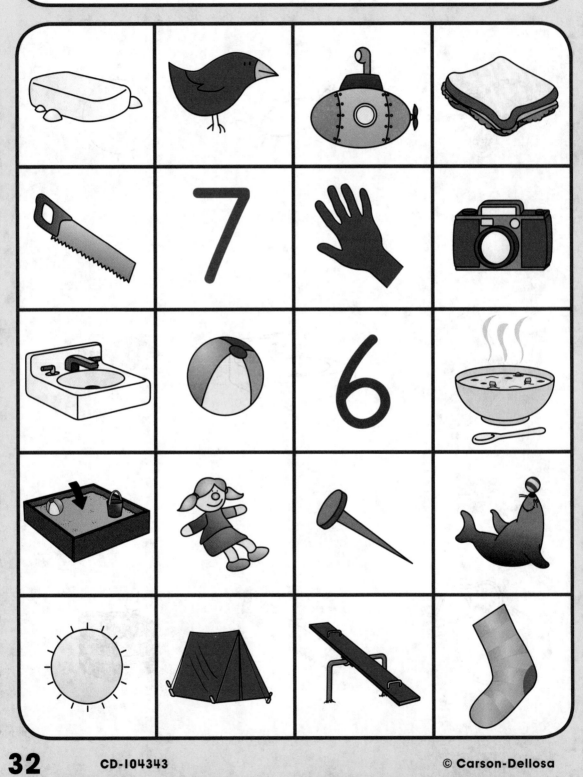

CD-104343

Say the name of each picture. Circle each picture that begins with the t sound.

Say the name of each picture. Circle each picture that begins with the **v** sound.

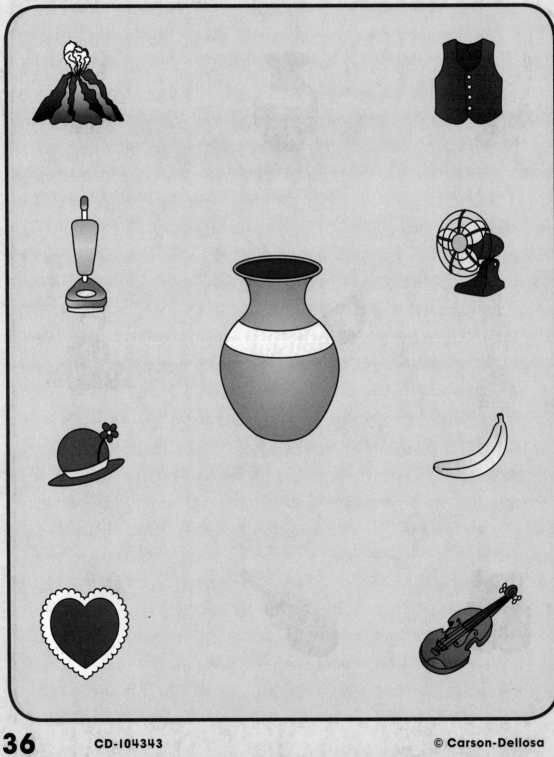

Say the name of each picture. Circle the beginning letter of each word.

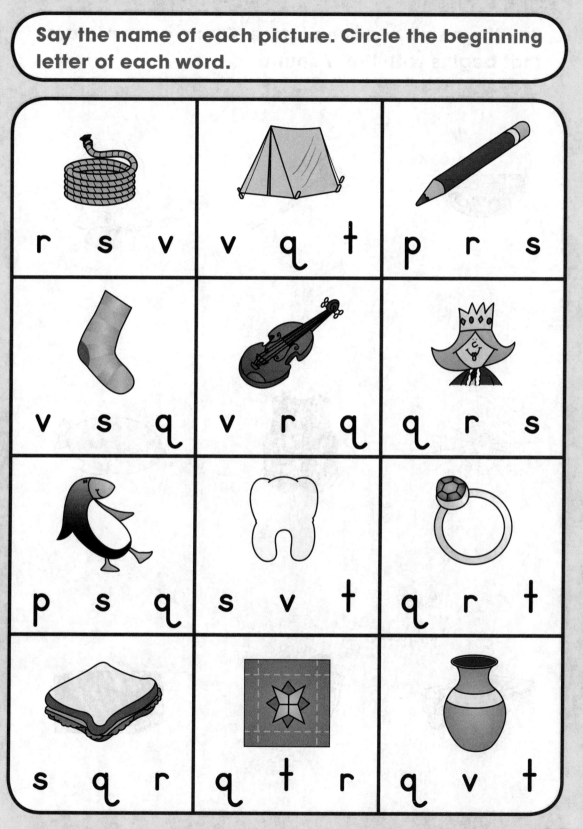

r s v	v q t	p r s
v s q	v r q	q r s
p s q	s v t	q r t
s q r	q t r	q v t

Say the name of each picture. Circle each picture that begins with the **w** sound.

CD-104343 © Carson-Dellosa

Say the name of each picture. Draw a line from the walrus to each picture that begins with the w sound.

Trace each letter y. Circle the picture in each row whose name begins with the y sound.

CD-104343 © Carson-Dellosa

Say the name of each picture. Circle each picture that begins with the **y** sound.

CD-104343   **41**

Say the name of each picture. Circle each picture that begins with the **z** sound.

CD-104343 © Carson-Dellosa

Say the name of each picture. Draw a line from the zebra to each picture that begins with the z sound.

Say the name of each picture. Circle the letter of the beginning sound.

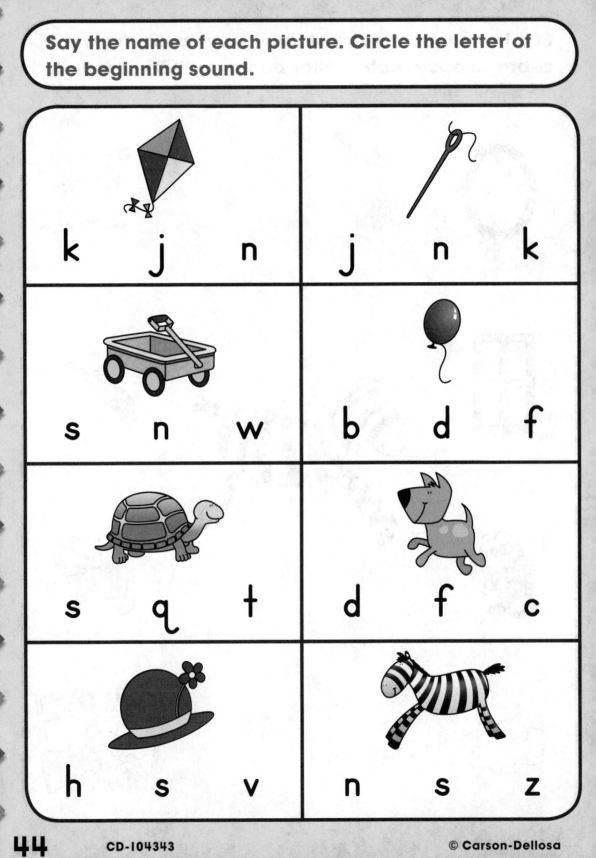

k   j   n

j   n   k

s   n   w

b   d   f

s   q   t

d   f   c

h   s   v

n   s   z

CD-104343

Say the name of each picture. Circle the letter of the beginning sound.

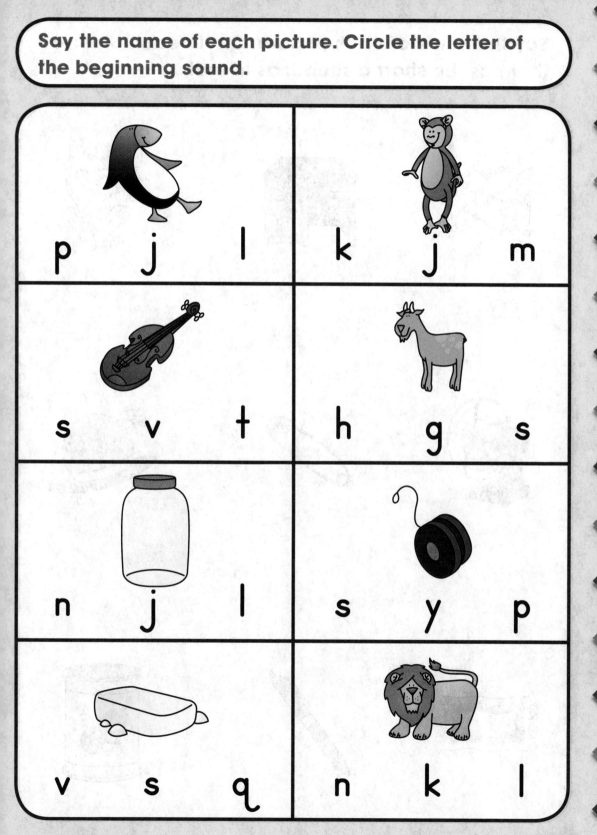

p   **j**   l

k   **j**   m

s   **v**   t

h   **g**   s

n   **j**   l

s   **y**   p

v   **s**   q

n   k   **l**

Say the name of each picture. Circle each picture that has the **short a** sound, as in **mat**.

CD-104343

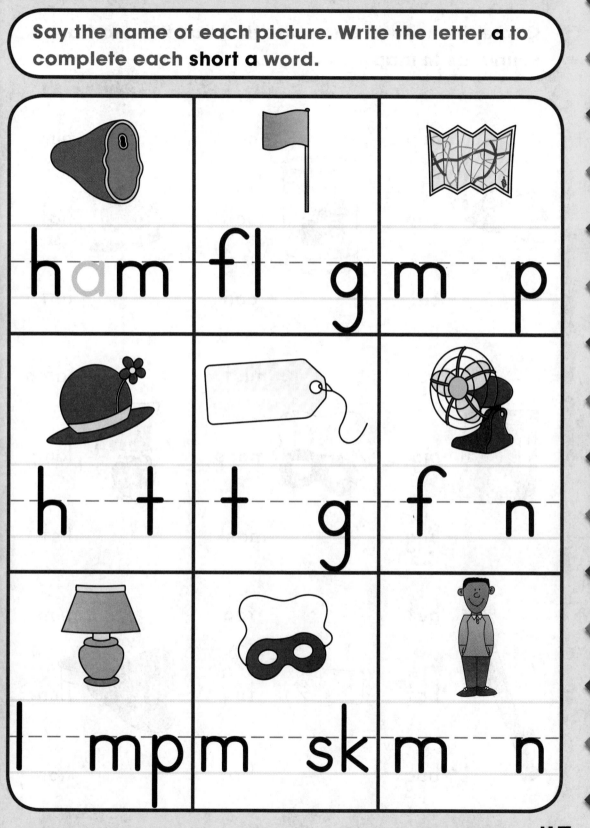

ham

fl___g

m___p

h___t

t___g

f___n

l___mp

m___sk

m___n

Circle the word in each box that has the **short a** sound, as in **map**.

cup	corn	him
cap	cob	hat
cut	can	hot
bag	mist	lamp
big	more	lump
bug	mask	list
bet	tag	him
bat	tug	hen
bug	tip	ham

Say the name of each picture. Circle each picture that has the **short e** sound, as in **egg**.

Say the name of each picture. Write the letter **e** to complete each **short e** word.

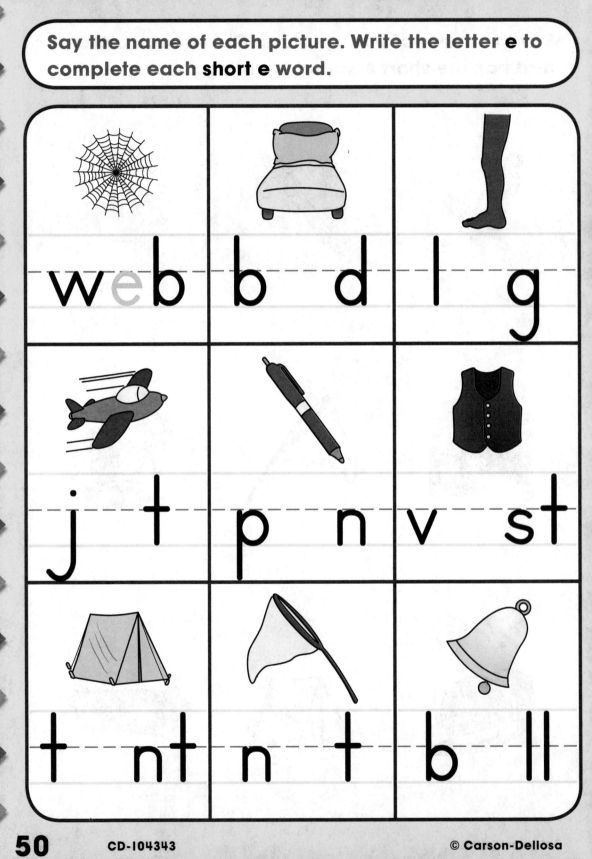

w e b   b _ d   l _ g

j _ t   p _ n   v _ st

t _ n t   n _ t   b _ ll

CD-104343   © Carson-Dellosa

Circle the word in each box that has the **short e** sound, as in **egg**.

pin	dress	not
pen	drip	nut
pat	drain	net

slid	bell	disk
sled	bolt	desk
slide	ball	dear

lag	ton	vest
leg	tint	vast
lit	tent	vat

 CD-104343

Say the name of each picture. Circle each picture that has the **short i** sound, as in **fin**.

CD-104343 © Carson-Dellosa

Say the name of each picture. Write the letter **i** to complete each **short i** word.

b i b   k _ t   p _ n

f _ sh   k _ ng   d _ sh

ch _ n   w _ g   s _ x

Circle the word in each box that has the **short i** sound, as in **fish**.

fun

fish

fan

---

pin

pan

peg

---

laps

lips

luck

---

key

king

kite

---

chin

can

cup

---

sunk

sand

sink

---

six

sax

sand

6

---

wag

went

wing

---

wig

wag

wash

   CD-104343

Say the name of each picture. Circle each picture that has the **short o** sound, as in **box**.

Say the name of each picture. Write the letter o to complete each **short o** word.

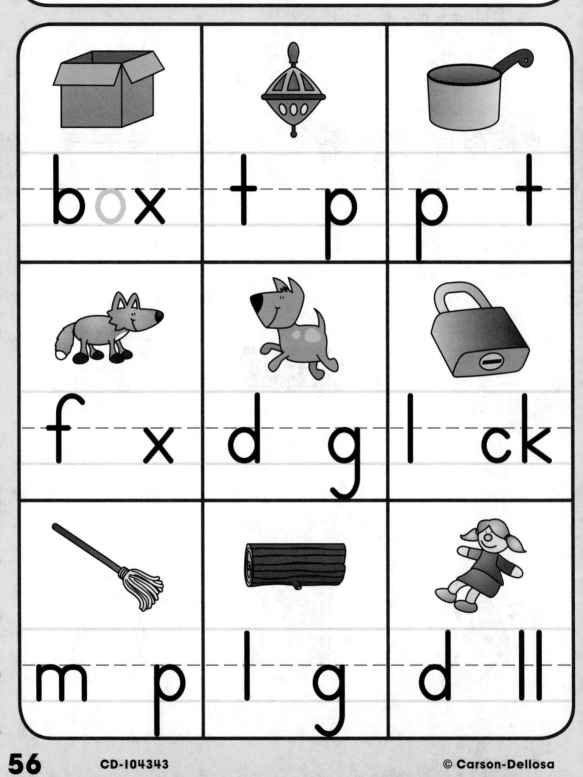

b o x   t p   p t

f   x   d g   l   ck

m   p   l g   d   ll

CD-104343   © Carson-Dellosa

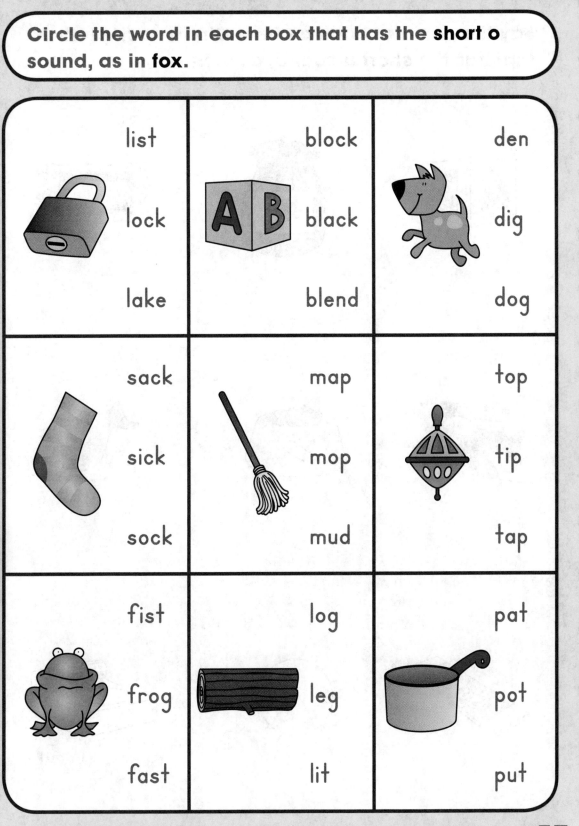

list

lock

lake

block

black

blend

den

dig

dog

sack

sick

sock

map

mop

mud

top

tip

tap

fist

frog

fast

log

leg

lit

pat

pot

put

Say the name of each picture. Circle each picture that has the **short u** sound, as in **bus**.

CD-104343

© Carson-Dellosa

Say the name of each picture. Write the letter **u** to complete each **short u** word.

c u p   r   g   t   b

s   n   d r   m   n   t

d   ck   h   t   m   g

CD-104343

Circle the word in each box that has the **short u** sound, as in **cub**.

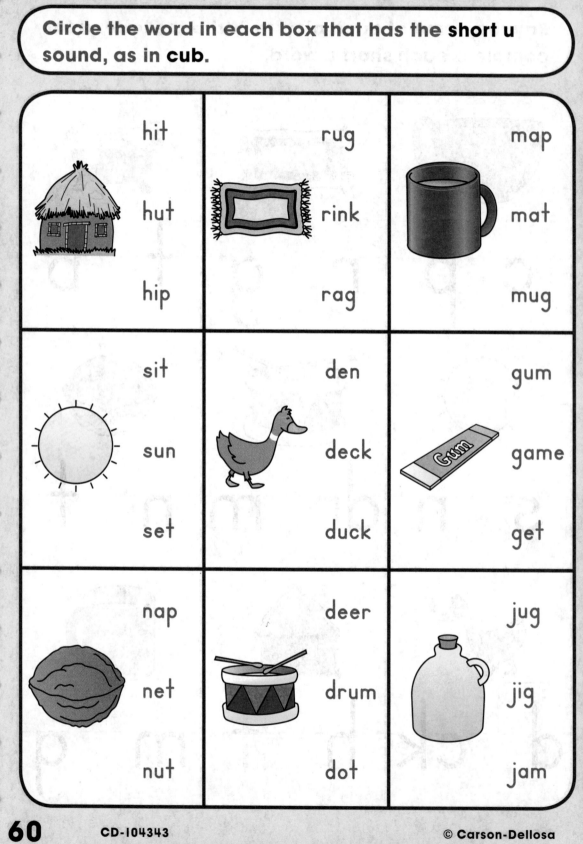

hit

hut

hip

rug

rink

rag

map

mat

mug

sit

sun

set

den

deck

duck

gum

game

get

nap

net

nut

deer

drum

dot

jug

jig

jam

60